AF454145

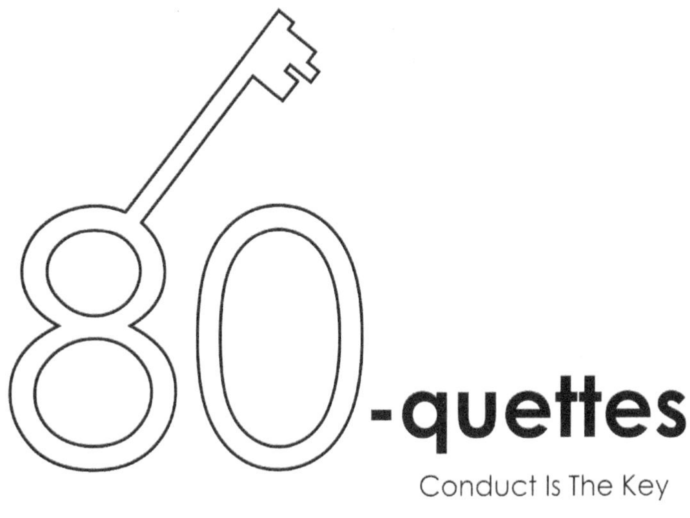

80-quettes

Conduct Is The Key

By Pratik Bharat Palor

Copyright © 2021 By Pratik 'BHARAT' Palor

This is a work of Self-help. Names, characters, businesses, places, events and incidents are either products of the author's imagination or used in a fictitious manner. Any resemblance to actual persons, living or dead, or actual events is purely coincidental.
All Rights Reserved

First Edition: Februay 2021
Printed in India

Printed at Dhote Offset Printer, Mumbai
Typeset in Batang

ISBN: 978-93-90267-69-9

Cover Design: Jaya Lokhande

STORYMIRROR
Stories that reflect you

Publisher: StoryMirror Infotech Pvt. Ltd.
      145, First Floor, Powai Plaza, Hiranandani Gardens,
      Powai, Mumbai - 400076, India

Web: https://storymirror.com
Facebook: https://facebook.com/storymirror
Twitter: https://twitter.com/story_mirror
Instagram: https://instagram.com/storymirror

❝ "Manners Maketh Man" and manners and/ or etiquettes are the cornerstones of civility. What we derive from ages of evolution of the human civilization, ultimately gets enshrined in the basic behavioral attributes that present the distinction between homo-sapiens and rest of the primate species. Application of the same could be improved if a person had access to the basic guidelines that would help not only prevent a conflict but also enhance a relationship into a beautiful bond. My dear friend Pratik has ventured into this territory and this book is a great work in laying the foundations for respectful, courteous, and harmonious interactions between two human beings, across different junctures of life. This book is a beacon that would help all navigate through different relationships in life, in the most tranquil manner."

Retired Wing Commander Sumit Kapoor has been a Navigator in the transport fleet of the Indian Air Force. He is also an Alumni of IIM Bangalore and Toulouse Business School, France and is at present working as Director – Business Development in an aviation startup. He is a certified scuba diver, a keen golfer and an avid writer himself.

 # THEY AGREE!

" Etiquettes are the building blocks of any civilization. They apply to almost every aspect of life. As social beings, it is essential for us to conduct ourselves, in a socially acceptable manner. In this era of globalization, marked by the constant changes and evolution, '80-quettes' will guide us towards an apt human behavior, thereby promoting understanding and fostering respect for distinct people and cultures."

Shailly Shah is the Founder & Editor of 'The Social Jigsaw' a socio-cultural magazine, published annually in English, since January 2020. Born and brought up in Calcutta, she has graduated in the field of Sociology (Hons.) from Calcutta University. Besides having a Master's Degree in Sociology and a UGC NET Qualification, Shailly has also done Master of Business Administration with Specializations in Marketing & HR. Belonging to a family having an educational, literary and cultural background, she is blessed with the opportunity to come across, various aspects of the society as a whole.

 # For & From Them

This is for my Parents, who have very carefully and attentively taught me how to behave and conduct myself. They fed me with manners and discipline like a daily meal. For them, etiquettes have always been the highest priority and I cannot thank them enough for it.

And a big bow of gratitude to all my professional seniors who have put all the efforts to shape me into the best possible.

66 Here is a 'life hack' guide that is packed with thoughtful little details to handle yourself with ease, tact and grace through myriad situations that are personal, social or professional. '80-quettes' lays the foundation of proper etiquette that cost nothing but mean everything. With a simple and straightforward approach, the author weaves the living fabric of society. If each of us practices these small and large considerations with those around us, the domino effect will be making life beautiful for all of us."

Dr Suchitra Kaul Misra is a Doctor of Philosophy who has a passion for therapeutic humor, healing and poetry. She is Chairperson Karnataka of ALL Ladies League and President Karnataka, Wellness & Wellbeing at WICCI – Women's Indian Chamber of Commerce and Industry. Author, poet and Distinguished Toastmaster with Toastmasters International, she has served on the Board of 3 Public Listed Companies and was recently recognized as 'Leader of the Decade' by the global Women Economic Forum 2020. She is the Honorary Board Member of IJBST Journal group. Founder of 'Dr Suchitra's Healing Garden' in Bengaluru, she offers integrated healing with laughter therapy to a spectrum of networks, ranging from corporate and educational institutions to NGO's and disadvantaged groups.

66 I have gone through the Manual for Human Behavior prepared by Pratik 'Bharat' Palor. It is a very significant work done by him. We all feel that these are necessary in every walk of our life, but we ignore them. In our old Scriptures, Sages have emphasized on three points while we behave, which are –

1. *Paatra* (Person)
2. *Kaal* (Time)
3. *Sthaan* (Place)

Pratik has discussed these three points in three segments as – People, Positions and Places. These points are covered in a very interesting manner. The reader will love to read, enjoy and learn them."

Mr. Pramod Shah is a Practicing CA. His articles on various subjects have been published in several magazines, journals and newspapers of the country. He has edited many social and cultural magazines, participated in T.V. talks and Radio talks. He is the Past President of "All India Marwari Yuva Manch" – devoted to socio-cultural activities having more than 650 branches and more than 50 thousand members throughout the country. He has organized and addressed more than 100 Seminars, Mushairas and Kavi Sammelans. He has written, compiled and edited numerous books.

“ This book is different, very different! Firstly, there is a deep thought behind the conceptualization of this book. Secondly, the way it has been written is pretty concise and crisp. Another good part is that the book is so individualistic in terms of its chapters that one may simply skip to any chapter based on the requirement. This is not a book which you read and keep in your library, but a reference document for any given situation that you are in. I believe, Pratik has done a fantastic job authoring this book. The generous idea behind is to help those who have never been taught about these things in the academic books or have never come across these kinds of situations. The book comes with a lot of practical experience of the author, so far as I have known his life.”

Amit Jain, married to Heena and father of two, is a Chartered Accountant and a Company Secretary. He has worked with international brands like Tata, Marriott and currently working with Suzlon and settled at Chicago, USA. He and Pratik studied together during their articleship for Chartered Accountancy. Besides being Pratik's personal consultant, Amit has been a behavior coach and a motivational speaker during his corporate stint with Marriott and Suzlon.

 # Well Begun!

स्वरदायिनी माँ शारदे को कोटिश नमन!

विघ्नहर्ता लम्बोदर गणपति को साष्टांग प्रणाम!

भक्तवल्लभ अकारण-कृपालु सियावर रामचन्द्र की जय!

सतत मार्गदर्शक-सखा-रक्षक पूर्णावतार श्री कृष्ण की जय!

One of the many things that differentiate humans from other creatures, is etiquettes. These are the unwritten rules or say best practices, developed over a long evolution of civilization. These rules define whether your behavior or conduct will be considered as appropriate or otherwise. These are also subject to the people, culture and environment you are in, at the moment. That's right, etiquettes do change their levels, types and acceptance depending upon the situation. An etiquette in a rich place can be termed as show off in a poor one. And an etiquette in a poor place can be considered absurd in a rich one. Etiquettes are not limited to but include your appearance, communication, expressions and body language.

This is the one thing that is capable of highlighting your minor deficiencies and also hide your major excellence. It can both cover and expose you. If the first impression is the last impression, etiquettes are going to decide the intensity and depth of that impression. You can win or lose people just with your mannerism or conduct. And it's something to adjust and adapt, as per the need of the moment. There is not one, straight and all-season formula to apply. Rather, there are people, positions and places to understand and behave accordingly.

It's not possible to behave most appropriately without sensing the environment, which includes the event, people, timing, place, culture and your own position amidst all. Only by gauging those, one can figure out how to act and react. It's all about being self-aware so that you don't fall prey to your own waves of emotion and thus maintain the balance and decorum. It can also be simplified as the behavior that you would expect from others. However, it's easier preached than practiced.

It's neither about pleasing anyone nor about intimidate oneself, but only about carrying yourself well in the company of any person or at a certain place or in a situation. Etiquettes must never be misconstrued as being submissive or compromising one's best interest. Rather, it is the most efficient tool to win your ground without the need of being aggressive. It gives you the edge in approaching people and driving things to the most optimum direction. And its absence can certainly have a negative impact, irrespective of your position or status or abilities. All human beings are judgmental and it's a fact to accept, rather than argue about. With the right etiquettes, you can always sway the judgment towards the most positive. And thereby define your positive terms with people.

The most common of etiquettes to be followed consistently with all, are as under:
   a. Greeting people, as you meet them, as per their age, position and the customs.
   b. Speak softly, politely and with respect.
   c. Allow others to speak and listen to them carefully, before responding.
   d. Attempt to remember names and salutations of people, as they appreciate a specific address.

e. Avoid staring at someone, especially a woman.

f. Follow the queue, whenever and wherever instructed to.

g. Ask and clarify, when in doubt, rather than assuming something and leading to confusion.

h. Maintain a safe and reasonable social distance with strangers.

However, in this book, we will be discussing and learning very specific things to follow.

Etiquettes are mostly simply explained in the phrase "behave same as you expected others to behave". Not that this is your first opportunity to learn etiquettes. We start to learn etiquettes from our family and friends, from a very tender age. But, all of us don't behave the same way in the same situations, in front of the same people and in the same places. Simply because our friends and family are not the same. Beyond that you must have read about some etiquettes at different places, but not all of those together, structurally compiled in the form of a book. In that case, how would you maintain the best of your decorum everywhere and every time? Who would tell you the right etiquettes and help you with the most appropriate behavior? I am attempting to be the one, by sharing both the recommendations and cautions.

– Wishing you a wonderful public life

Pratik 'Bharat' Palor (Darpan)

Note: The people, positions and places mentioned in each chapter may come as a combination also; which would require combined application of the recommendations mentioned for each of those.

HANDLE
WITH CARE

S. N.	Segment	Topic	Page
1		With Elders	25
2		With Youngsters	29
3		With Kids & Toddlers	33
4		With Strangers	37
5		With Neighbors	41
6		With Elderly	45
7	People Related	With Relatives	49
8		With Guests	53
9		With the Differently Abled	57
10		With Subordinates	61
11		With Superiors	65
12		With Friends	69
13		With Colleagues	73

35		At Movie Theatre	173
36		At Social Media	177
37		At Workplace	181
38		At Foreign Trips	185
39		At Tourist Places	189

Jigyāsa is the girl next door, who loves to learn through inquiry and experiences. She was curious to know how to conduct herself in order to win people and situations.

Every time she encounters a doubt, she asks her mother "How To?" and her mother explains...

This time it's about human behavior...

SEGMENT A :

PEOPLE RELATED

Jigyâsa (more upset than curious): "Generation gap is a bitter reality and you too are a party to it, Mumma!"

Veda: "Fair enough. Let's talk about it and understand the source of this gap."

Jigyâsa: "The source is never ending expectations and never hearing attitude, right..."

 # With Elders

All of us are flocked by elders and pretty much brought up by them. Elders include our parents, grand-parents, family members and their friends. They bring us support, experience, advice and care, for free. At times, they tolerate our tantrums and improper behavior also. They, out of genuine concern for our wellbeing, share all they can, whether materialistic or psychological. They try to both guide us and cover / protect us in the different and difficult situations of life. Elders have gone through possibly all what we do and hence definitely have some important tips to share. In most cases, they are not technically as sound and upgraded as we are, but life is less about technology and more about soft skills, which they have in plenty.

They may come across occasionally and at times may be strangers also. At times, they might get bit possessive and burden you with expectations too, but again that's something to talk about and not retaliate. They will sure have their own deficiencies and failures, which can be utilized as a learning to build upon.

✓ Tell them that they are important to you and you need them.

✓ Appreciate their contribution to your life, even if it's limited to just an occasional advice.

✓ Remind them of some healthy, jovial and worthy memories.

✓ Seek their advice whenever you get stuck and don't happen to find a way.

✓ Share your plans with them and try to make them a party to it.

✓ Constantly communicate with them, even without any agenda.

✗ Rejecting their ideas or suggestions, by terming those as not relevant.

✗ Refusing to talk to them or making excuses like being too busy to connect.

✗ Not allowing them to share some tips of life from their experiences.

✗ Disrespecting them as an individual and hurting their self-esteem.

✗ Not acknowledging their efforts and willingness to support you.

✗ Neither participating in their plans nor inviting them to join you.

Jigyãsa was excited to learn and reacted: "This is so cool, Maa! Now I can't make a mistake."

Veda: "My pleasure Betu! Glad that you asked and I could share".

Jigyãsa: "So, what about youngsters..."

 # With Youngsters

As we grow, we get to meet youngsters who wish to spend time with us and learn from us. All our hits and misses can both entertain and inspire them. With a little comfort extended by us, they would love to get closer and have a friendly relationship with us. They are pretty curious and ready to experiment, which is the best opportunity for us to share our thoughts and provoke interesting ideas in them. They are full of energy, urge, self-motivation, ambition and willingness to do great things.

Youngsters may have different areas of interest and ideas of execution, but they are always hungry for direction. They don't like to be pushed or confronted, but always welcome someone to look up to. They are not corrupted or manipulated yet, and hence receive things as they are. And in today's world, they have all the power to create, mould, re-direct, change and drive things. A little appreciation, respect and empathy can build wonderful relations with them. They may have superior or inferior skills and competencies, but that's where the opportunity of coaching is.

✓ Appreciate their dreams, inclinations, choices and ways of working.

✓ Encourage them to follow their heart, with the necessary caution and direction.

✓ Learn from their technological upgrades and make them feel good about it.

✓ Invite their ideas / suggestions / advices in the relatively larger and serious matters of life.

✓ Stay connected and friendly, to ensure and sustain the relation of mutual trust.

✓ Extend some responsibilities, freedom and decision-making power to them.

- ✘ Making irrelevant comparisons with some known or unknown successful person.

- ✘ Showing no interest towards their ambitions or ideas of success in life.

- ✘ Giving them decisions, rather than advice / tips / insights out of experiences.

- ✘ Neglecting their inputs or recommendations to deal with a situation.

- ✘ Counting their failures just too many times and without any contribution to correct those.

- ✘ Humiliating them in front of relatives / friends / teachers / neighbors.

Jigyàsa: "Fair enough and I think you have been treating me well."

Veda: "Oh really! Thanks for the appreciation".

Jigyàsa: "But, I still want to know how to deal with small kids..."

 With Small Kids

Innocence, mischief, nothing to remember, nothing to hate, no worries, irrational gut feel, complaints with constantly deleted history, no selfish motives, crankiness for no reason, deep desire of love & care, nothing to gain or lose, no planning or preparations and yet all of it falls short to define kids and toddlers. In true sense, they live in the present and anything beyond that doesn't exist. They have curiosity of the highest order. And they enjoy themselves. May be that's why people say that kids are miniatures of God.

Since their brain and body are shaping up, they are very agile and eager to explore things. A lot of careful and focused attention is required for them, as they haven't yet learnt to take care of themselves. They can laugh and cry without getting tired. They can slip, trip and fall many times, with the exact same sequence of events. Their highest priorities are food, sleep and play, which they effortlessly make the priorities of everyone around them. That's precisely why we often wish to become kids again.

✓ Handle them with the utmost care, both physically and psychologically.

✓ Tell them inspiring, healthy, happy, brave and kind stories.

✓ Encourage them to be strong and feel strong, so that they grow up quicker.

✓ Make them independent for all tasks and situations, at the earliest possible.

✓ Give them support & cover, in all conditions, irrespective of how confident they are.

✓ Teach them to humbly accept success and also appreciate failure, however small it may be.

* Making fun of them for the small things that they cannot manage.

* Developing fear of the unknown and imaginary devil, in order to manage their tantrums.

* Assuming them to be emotionally unaware and thus ignoring their feelings / indications.

* Allowing anyone to disrespect their childhood and fragile mind.

* Scolding them when they cannot even understand their mistake.

* Expecting them to behave, while they are not some toys but small playful humans.

Jigyâsa: "Awww, so cute they are and yes we need to be very careful and caring with them."

Veda: "Exactly! They have feelings but are dependent for everything else."

Jigyâsa: "Can you tell me about strangers also! I feel quite nervous in front of them..."

 # With Strangers

Strangers are those who are not known or familiar to you and vice versa. For this very reason, they expect you to maintain a safe and reasonable distance with them. While there may be opportunities and reasons for you to solicit introduction and get familiar with strangers, there are socially acceptable ways and means to approach them. Due to being strangers, they might have strange and unexpected reactions to your actions. There are chances of them welcoming you as you are, but the probability of that happening is much lower.

Strangers have unknown personality traits, priorities in life, importance attached to different things, sensitivities, biases, perceptions, likes, dislikes, attitude, etc. In addition to that, there may be cultural and environmental factors in play, while dealing with strangers. Making it comfortable with them is the only way to reap appreciable results. Strangers may not stay long in your life, but their impact can be. Your actions and their reactions can probably lead to a lot of pleasant or unpleasant situations.

✓ Address them appropriately and with due respect, as per their age and position.

✓ Respect their space, privacy, freedom and also the individuality.

✓ Remember to show gratitude on receiving a favor or assistance.

✓ Avoid a discussion on any sensitive subject, whether personal, social or political.

✓ Gently and humbly offer them food / eatables, without insisting on having it.

✓ Extend a help to the extent possible, whether in terms of sharing a fact or thing.

✖ Judging them for their looks, attire, language and/or mannerism.

✖ Trying to get friendly and encroaching into their personal space / time.

✖ Giving them advice / suggestion without them asking for it.

✖ Being too loud with them or around them, and thereby irritating them.

✖ Asking random questions and not allowing them to focus on what they wish to do.

✖ Provoking or entering into an argument which may not lead anywhere.

Jigyāsa: "That means I need to be cautious and confident at the same time."

Veda: "Precisely. And also maintain a safe distance, till the time you get to know them well."

Jigyāsa: "How about the neighbors, who are always close to us, quite literally…"

 With Neighbors

Literally, the people closest to you are your neighbors. May or may not be close at heart, but they are certainly by existence. They can quickly become your dearest and most approachable friends or the most undesirable people in life. They may have the same standard of life as your, or acutely different also. They may be in living the same stage of life or ahead or behind you. They may or may not enjoy the same kind of food, entertainment, leisure, company, festivals etc.

Neighbors may choose to avoid each other, but they better not do that. With all the possible differences or commonalities, neighbors breathe in the very same air and share some common space. Willingly or otherwise, you have to connect with them and, at times, share things. There are certain expectations, mostly related to situations of emergency, which neighbors have with each other. There are few occasions when you have only your neighbors to share your joy or sorrow with. There are many things to learn from and teach to a neighbor, provided you are in good terms with them.

✓ Reach out to them and greet them well on your first meeting.

✓ Exchange basic info about each other, which can come handy as a neighbor.

✓ Assure them of security and privacy at all times, from your side.

✓ Maintain a friendly / family relationship with them, to enjoy the mutual comfort.

✓ Join them in their celebrations and invite them for yours.

✓ Support them in difficult / challenging situations, when nobody can reach sooner.

✘ Repeatedly approaching them for your grocery kind of requirements.

✘ Playing loud music at odd time and penalizing them for staying close to you.

✘ Getting involved in pity fights between their child and yours.

✘ Making irrational complaints and not sorting out their complaints, if any.

✘ Backbiting or gossiping about them to your other neighbors.

✘ Blocking or obstructing their way to home or the parking space.

Jigyāsa: "Wow! If treated well, they can really be our best friends, without being termed so."

Veda: "Yes, indeed. And there are even closer friends back home, whom we tend to ignore."

Jigyāsa: "Who! And how can we ignore friends..."

 With Elderly

They have lived it thoroughly and feel happy to see you grow. They need consistent support and empathy, for which they look forward to you. They are very slow in everything they do, especially communication, but keen to do all that they can. They expect and deserve respect and care. Their life is filled with emotions and a sense of slow-moving time. Survival is what takes most of their otherwise meek energy. Memories are their companions, which, however, often make them feel lonely and empty. They have observed few people dying, who belonged to the same age group.

There are a very few, in that age, who can keep themselves up and have the luxury of not being bed-ridden. Unlike others, there are those rare and lucky ones who could plan for this age, have a relatively healthy body and things to do. Otherwise, medicines and physical weakness make them irritated, to be topped up with the ignoring eyes of people surrounding them. Not being relevant to anyone is extremely painful, for sure. It's tough, yet important to make them feel comfortable

✓ Make them feel respected and cared about, as that's all what they need.

✓ Always be around and available for them, as much as for small kids.

✓ Take care of their food and medical needs, since they cannot.

✓ Bring them to every possible event of celebration that makes them feel alive.

✓ Have conversations with them, even if it happens to be one sided.

✓ Seek their confirmation / concurrence for things, even if it doesn't really matter.

* Making them feel lonely, redundant and irrelevant for the family.

* Not attending to their calls / needs or making an assistance available to them.

* Treating them like a lifeless stuff in the house and not showing any interest in their being.

* Leaving them at an old age home, with no recourse to the family.

* Getting irritated with their physical and mental state of health.

* Keeping them in isolation and thereby drying them up emotionally.

Jigyāsa: "Never before I could relate so much to them. Yes, we tend to ignore them."

Veda: "Let's correct it. As they say, better late than never. You know what! They are quick in responding."

Jigyāsa: "Is it! I mostly find few others quite responsive or say reactive..."

 # With Relatives

Tough to define them. They come with so many varieties of connection, age, culture, thoughts, experiences, abilities, intentions and what not. Yet, they always come with expectations, whether you happen to be the guest or the host. Relatives may be known or half known or distant or alien. They may or may not remember your name or interests and vice versa. They can get quite judgmental and absolutely uninterested, at times. They can suddenly ask you for some help and you will have no choice but to oblige.

Relatives are a great channel of grapevines in the family and therefore able to make or mar your image. This must not be taken as a threat, but as an opportunity and tool to your benefit. Understanding their thought process, influence and impact can be tricky, but managing them is not that difficult. They mostly come in contact at less frequency and for a short period of time, but there may be situations otherwise too. You will always have that one relative who has contributed well to your life and the contrast cases too.

✓ Stay aware and connected with them, whether living in proximity or not.

✓ Visit them occasionally, especially when invited to attend a celebration or condolence.

✓ Invite them to share your special and/or tough moments in life.

✓ Seek their advice / support in matters that they champion, whether professional or personal.

✓ Advance assistance to them, to the extent possible.

✓ Appreciate and enjoy their or their family's success, like your own.

✗ Interfering in their personal and family matters, without their consent or intent.

✗ Asking them for undue favors in personal and/or professional life.

✗ Manipulating discussions or words to put them in a spot.

✗ Making financial comparisons and putting them in an embarrassing / uncomfortable situation.

✗ Passing unpleasant comments on the academic / professional performance of their children.

✗ Giving unsolicited advice, mixed with criticism, when it's not even appreciated.

Jigyâsa: "I get the point. We too are relatives
and must know how to behave."

Veda: "Specially when you visit them, or they
come to visit you."

Jigyâsa: "You mean guests! It takes so much to
entertain them, right..."

 With Guests

Whether invited or otherwise, whether acquainted or strangers, whether expected or not, whether visiting for a quick meet or stay; guests do come with well-defined and several expectations. Being guests, provide them several obvious privileges. In fact, the *Bharatiy* traditions and values recommend for the highest of respect, welcome and hospitality for any guests, whosoever they may be. We must always prepare well for the expected guests and not fumble in front of the unexpected ones.

Guests rightfully share food, shelter, amenities and, at times, emotions also. We need to be very careful in sharing or exposing our feelings with the guests, depending upon our level of confidence and bonding with them. Guests are not only an opportunity to connect and build network, but also a responsibility to maintain a good relation and impression. They can easily channelize a great amount of perception about us and our perception about many others.

✓ Greet them well and make them comfortable for the time that they are staying with you.

✓ Share your resources with them, according to the purpose of their visit.

✓ Recall, share and create memorable moments with them.

✓ Serve them exclusive dishes, which may be their choice or your specialty.

✓ Accommodate your schedule to attend them and fulfill their purpose of visit.

✓ Give them a gentle send-off to encourage them visiting again and inviting you too.

✗ Giving them a hint that they are not welcome and must leave early.

✗ Treating them or their kids poorly or not with due respect.

✗ Talking ill about them or complaining about others in front of them.

✗ Complaining about or insulting your / their kids in their presence.

✗ Pushing your choices of food, entertainment or travel on them.

✗ Ignoring their presence and time or excusing yourself on account of being busy.

Jigyāsa: "I can actually recall all the great memories that we created as hosts or guests."

Veda: "Do you also remember the special child who had visited us, along with your cousin?"

Jigyāsa: "Yes, I do. And till date I am not sure how to treat such a person..."

With the Differently Abled

Those suffering with any physical or mental disability; however, having their energy, power and abilities concentrated in something else, which may be another limb or sense or intellect. While they continue to attempt to be independent, motivated and confident; it's difficult for them and needs relatively extra efforts. There are several examples around us, who have achieved extraordinary feats in life, despite their struggle with such disabilities. And there is a large number of those who are not able to make both ends meet.

What they expect from everyone, including their family and friends, is a sense of empathy and support. Sympathy is derogatory and disrespectful for them, whether they are in a position to express that or not. Trusting and augmenting their capabilities is what heals their otherwise irrecoverable condition.

✓ Show confidence in their abilities, which they themselves may not have.

✓ Encourage them to challenge their limitations and aim big in life.

✓ Support them with physical and/or psychological aids to enable them stand strong.

✓ Appreciate their willingness to do things and also their efforts / success.

✓ Introduce them to others with dignity, respect and pride.

✓ Accept them as an equal or, at times, more able and strong human being.

* Making them feel weak / dependent / helpless / unfortunate / unwanted.

* Offering them help / support / assistance, even when they don't need or ask for it.

* Making fun of them or indirectly humiliating them for their apparent limitations.

* Not giving them deserving opportunities to demonstrate and prove themselves.

* Reminding them of what they are not capable of, rather than boosting their confidence.

* Isolating them from the general life or people and pushing them into loneliness.

Jigyâsa: "You are right. They don't need sympathy, but empathy and belief."

Veda: "Absolutely! You must always contribute to their self-confidence and abilities."

Jigyâsa: "And, I am sure that you are doing the same with the people who work with you..."

 With Subordinates

A set of people, who report to you and support you in fulfilling the goals and objectives of an organization which is owned or served by you. They may or may not be younger and/or less qualified and/or less experienced, within the same industry or otherwise, than you. Furthermore, they may have different cultural, financial and emotional backgrounds. Their alignment or commitment towards the organizational goals may also be higher or lower.

It's important to understand and fulfill their needs, whether personal or professional, in order to stimulate their efforts and loyalty. As mentioned, and emphasized by many studies, researches and management coaches, human resources are by far the strongest elements of any organization. People can make or mar the potential fate of any organization. Irrespective of the marketing and advertising efforts made otherwise, they are the most visible, vocal and trusted ambassadors of any organization; for the public at large.

✓ Set clear goals / objectives and provide them the resources to achieve those.

✓ Remember to credit them for the small and big success at workplace.

✓ Maintain a personal connect, beyond the work and professional relationship.

✓ Encourage and allow them to think of better ways to work and suggest solutions.

✓ Recognize their endurance, commitment, will and efforts; beyond the results achieved.

✓ Help them grow in their career, whether within the same or a different organization.

✖ Assuming them to be lazy, ignorant, unwilling and in lack of energy.

✖ Not giving them enough of freedom, support and decision-making power to execute work.

✖ Giving strong feedback in the presence of others and thereby demotivating them.

✖ Not making them part of a success story and keeping it limited to oneself.

✖ Making it difficult for them to maintain a healthy work-life balance.

✖ Overloading them with work and eventually proving them to be under-performing.

Jigyāsa: "Got it! It's important to make them feel valued and important for the organization."

Veda: "Correct! That's when they can relate to the larger objective and give their best."

Jigyāsa: "One day I will have a team to lead and follow these tips. But, how about those above me..."

 With Superiors

For all practical purposes and irrespective of the work culture practiced, they are the seniors at workplace. They possess the experience, expertise, wisdom and management skills, which are more seasoned and hence deserve a lot of respect. Their willingness to guide, coach, mentor and support must always be welcomed and honored. Their occasional harshness or aggression may be taken in a positive sense, since they bear and sustain through relative greater pressures and responsibilities.

They often face the prejudices, lack of trust and negative emotions of their subordinates. This can be caused by lack of communication from either side, grapevine prevalent in the organization, pre-conceived notions, a history of not so pleasant conversations and/or limited opportunities to connect. While the greater responsibilities to solve such a situation is with the manager, the subordinates are also required to come forward and speak up for themselves, in a situation of doubt, difficulty or conflict.

✓ Understand their viewpoint before concluding anything otherwise.

✓ Reach out to them for any challenges / trouble, rather than keeping it with yourself.

✓ Align you actions with their thoughts and plans, so that they will stand with you.

✓ Ask questions, when in doubt; rather than making assumptions or maintaining a confusion.

✓ Be open for seeking their help, when stuck in a difficult situation.

✓ Appreciate that they possess the same or greater experience and eligibility to be there.

✘ Suffering from the prejudice that they are not fair and deserving to be on that position.

✘ Questioning their decisions or thought process, not in front of them but otherwise.

✘ Giving poor / bad / harsh feedback about them to the external world.

✘ Chasing them for a support in job change, when they move to another organization.

✘ Not giving them a fair feedback when you find them going the wrong way.

✘ Not supporting their cause with the expected level of energy, effort and commitment.

Jigyâsa: "We may not agree always, but it's a must to understand their perspective, right!"

Veda: "Wonderful! You could summarize it so well and completely."

Jigyâsa: "That's because I have few people in my life who often act like a boss. You know who..."

 # With Friends

Our partners in every emotion, however personal it may be. They know us deeply well, at times more than our parents or even spouse. They come forward for any kind of support and stand by us in the most difficult situations, irrespective of their personal challenges or limitations. They extend the moral and emotional support that can help us sail through any turmoil. They are the source and shield of our self-esteem. Our secrets and hidden feelings are their personal possessions. Nobody, but a friend, can make us feel good about ourselves in the most depressing situations; even if it takes making fun of us.

And yes, they have all the right to expect the same from us. Friendship is the most mutually cared and garnered relation of all, since there is no involvement or interference of any third person in this. It has to be consistently nurtured and preserved by both, without any external help. And, that needs a lot of trust, intensity and solidarity at the same time.

✓ Stand by them in the places and situations where nobody else will.

✓ Keep their secrets when they don't even realize that you possess those.

✓ Stay informal with them, which is essential to this very relationship.

✓ Share your fair opinion / feedback / suggestion, which can guide and lead them.

✓ Stay connected even when you cannot continue to be physically close.

✓ Give them random visits and surprises at their special occasions to rejuvenate the memories.

✗ Opening their secrets to the people whom they don't intend to be aware of.

✗ Reaching out to them only for a support and not otherwise or without any purpose.

✗ Refusing, directly or indirectly, to assist them in a situation of trouble.

✗ Ignoring them when they are in a dire need of emotional or financial support.

✗ Giving them an advice which you don't believe to be true or helpful.

✗ Pulling them into ill habits, which may interrupt their education, profession or relationship.

Jigyâsa: "Yeah! They take the same liberty which I also enjoy with them."

Veda: "And the comfort also. Friends can, at times, become your guides and guardians also."

Jigyâsa: "I often wonder if I will find a friend at the workplace..."

 With Colleagues

Knowingly carving them out of the superiors and subordinates, who may be included in the same term from a dictionary meaning perspective. There are people who work with us, in the same organization, with or without a direct working relationship. They may be in a support function or customer functions or stakeholders. They might get in touch frequently, occasionally or rarely. Their needs or expectations or deliverables may be regular or intermittent.

Here are the people who can create and sustain a perception about you, in the organization. They do feel your presence and contribution, towards themselves and overall. And yes, you do reciprocate that for them. While working together for the common organizational goals, there are some mutual expectations, not limited to the working relationship but also including the mutual behavior and respect. At the end of the day, it's all professional and nothing personal.

✓ Appreciate and acknowledge their efforts for achieving the same common goal.

✓ Make them a partner in your deliverables and build the understanding of cooperation.

✓ Spend time with them beyond the work, to develop a personal connect.

✓ Participate with them in the occasional team building activities.

✓ Stand by them when they have a bad day at work or have to stretch / slog.

✓ Recognize and celebrate their work related and/or personal achievements.

✗ Indulging into baseless gossips that create and sustain unreasonable perceptions.

✗ Getting aggressive or loud in the situations of dissent or disagreement.

✗ Assuming them to be lacking the efforts, ability and caliber for recognition and growth.

✗ Giving a biased / skewed / selective feedback that impacts them negatively.

✗ Taking different stands at different occasions to make it difficult for the collective project.

✗ Differentiating between colleagues in terms of personal and/or professional treatment.

Jigyâsa: "Friendship at workplace can be quite valuable and productive."

Veda: "True. Be it workplace or home, you need to be watchful of your position and act accordingly."

Jigyâsa: "Does that mean the kind of role that I am playing, at a time..."

SEGMENT B : POSITION RELATED

Jigyāsa: "If I understand it correctly, I can be in various positions at different times or places."

Veda: "Right. Each position will have it's own profile to do justice with."

Jigyāsa: "To get into any position and be worth it, do I need to get trained first..."

# As a Trainee

When you wish to learn the desired skill(s) of a chosen field or a particular aspect of it, you seek that structured training from an expert who has the subject matter knowledge, experience and the art of transmitting the crux of it to you. Depending upon the skill and the trainer/coach/mentor/guide, it may be short or long, indoor, outdoor, remotely conducted, regular or need based, one-to-one or in a group, classroom type or fieldwork type, paid or free or a mix of all of these. As a trainee, one must have and showcase the elements of a student or disciple also.

While it is for the trainee or guardians or organization to choose a suitable trainer, once chosen, the trainer owns the training and the trainee, as well. In order to achieve the desired outcome of a training, one must constantly and completely dedicate oneself to the entire course of training, which may include pre-work and post training assignments. A training must be conducted and attended with the sheer thought of learning and not just completion, with or without a certificate.

✓ Believe in the ability and experience of your coach, in order to learn.

✓ Give the required / desired time and energy, as prescribed by your coach.

✓ Be consistent, punctual, disciplined and attentive towards the training.

✓ Clear your doubts and be sure about what you learn or understand.

✓ Apply your learning to practical situations and get back to your coach with the results.

✓ Identify your weak areas and reach out to your coach for specific guidance.

✘ Getting irritated with the tough tasks or training given by the coach.

✘ Making comparisons / judgments about the speed and efficiency of training.

✘ Taking the training casually and not appreciate its importance or impact.

✘ Not getting involved into it and just passing it through as a formality.

✘ Not asking the right questions, in order to work on your improvement areas.

✘ Ignoring the performance / progress feedback received from your coach.

Jigyâsa: "Thank God, I didn't enroll for any training before having a word with you."

Veda: "Nothing to be nervous about. Be a trainee or a trainer, you need to be self-aware and receptive."

Jigyâsa: "I often wonder how trainers prepare themselves and maintain that robust persona..."

 # As a Coach

Being chosen to be a coach for someone (including Trainer/Mentor/Guide, while the dictionary meanings may differ), is a great responsibility. There is someone trusting your command on the subject matter, relevant experience in applying the same, ability to structurally share it across and also solve the immediate or potential problems around it. In today's world, it becomes equally important to be upgraded and abreast with the technological advancements.

Both the trainee(s) and the sponsor of training (if a different person/organization) have certain expressed and/or hidden expectations from the training, which are completely dependent on the coach, provided there is due support from the trainee also. A coach must be aware and vigilant of that, throughout the training. It's not just the completion of training, but the future actions of the trainee(s) which would reflect what change the coach was able to bring about. And, in order to improvise, a coach has to welcome and accept feedback and inputs too.

✓ Give the constant best of your abilities to help your trainees learn.

✓ Treat all the trainees equally, with special focus to the bright ones.

✓ Make the training interactive and encourage them to freely participate.

✓ Stay open to learn from their innovative and un-orthodox ways.

✓ Keep updating the ways, methods, techniques and instruments of training.

✓ Acknowledge and respond to each query / doubt, however silly it might sound.

✖ Not extending the same training, support and guidance to all the trainees.

✖ Sticking to one way of coaching and not giving importance to the dynamic needs of trainees.

✖ Not leading by example, in terms of discipline, commitment and energy.

✖ Making it a one-way communication and dialogue to discourage exchange of ideas.

✖ Not seeking feedback on effectiveness of learning and challenges in application.

✖ Drawing comparisons and demotivating the from staying open to learn collectively.

Jigyāsa: "Indeed a great responsibility to develop and hone someone's skills, with your experience."

Veda: "Equally difficult and responsible job is to find out the right person for such a role."

Jigyāsa: "Who can screen and identify the best person to carry out a responsible role..."

 As an Interviewer

Executing the responsibility to choose the right (say the most suitable) candidate for a particular role in the organization, is not only important but testing one's own skills and competencies, at the same time. As an interviewer, one has to not only judge the credentials of a job seeker, but also showcase the organization culture and comprehensive maturity of oneself. An interviewer, whether individual or in a panel, is considered for this role assuming the ability to understand the critical aspects of a role profile and match it with the candidate.

Interviews may be conducted in different conditions and places. An interviewer needs to be composed, balanced and unbiased, with all the candidates. And, also remain focused on the needs of the organization. While a candidate is seeking a job, s/he is also a human being to be treated well. These aspects are critical for not only making them feel good and motivated, but also represent the organization very well, irrespective of the selection or rejection.

✓ Greet the interviewee well and make her / him comfortable for a conversation.

✓ Avoid any bias of appearance, language, accent, academic strength or origin.

✓ Carry a pleasant mood in the interview, to give a good impression of the work culture.

✓ Explore the strengths and weaknesses of the candidate from an assessment perspective.

✓ Provide enough of data if the question is about calculations or decision making.

✓ Let them walk back with a smile and self-belief, irrespective of how the interview went.

✘ Making it feel like an investigation into their academic / professional career.

✘ Not allowing them enough time to frame and complete their answers.

✘ Digging too much into a question, when you already realize that they don't know it.

✘ Asking personal questions / details, which may be offensive or sensitive.

✘ Frowning upon them for incorrect / not up to the mark kind of answers.

✘ Giving them hints of selection or rejection, during the interview.

Jigyâsa: "That must take a huge amount of experience and skills to pick the skilled people."

Veda: "It does. And that's why people prepare a lot and constantly to prove themselves."

Jigyâsa: "It's easy to talk to you and ask the questions that I want. But, how to answer questions..."

 # As an Interviewee

Looking forward to a job opportunity, recalling all what you have learnt through your academic and/or professional experience, honing your communication skills, building and sustaining a lot of confidence; you go for an interview. You would have already gone through a lot of articles, videos and personal / professional consultation on how to give it your best shot in an interview. You might also have an experience of cracking and not cracking several interviews. In fact, you might also have taken a few interviews yourself.

Despite all what you know about how to present ourselves in an interview, every interview happens to be different (and a harder nut to crack) from the earlier ones. This is not because you were less prepared, but because of the different and/or higher expectations from the interviewer. If you are being interviewed as a celebrity, the stage is all yours and there is no need to be nervous. However, you need to be careful in making any statement, since there are many people watching you to either for inspiration or for conspiracy.

✓ Research well about the organization and the interviewer, in advance.

✓ Be genuine, truthful, to the point and honest about your capabilities.

✓ Present yourself well, sober and professional; without overdoing on the dressing or looks.

✓ Think of a question to ask and ask it when the time or opportunity arises.

✓ Be gentle, calm and patient in both listening to the questions and responding to those.

✓ Feel free to drink some water if you feel thirsty and/or nervous.

✗ Attempting to impress the interviewer with your dressing, more than the answers.

✗ Trying to make up and push answers, when you are not even sure about it.

✗ Asking the interviewer whether your answers were right or wrong or the right answer.

✗ Getting too friendly or personal with the interviewer and trying to gain bonus points.

✗ Boasting about academic and/or professional achievements, beyond the relevance.

✗ Asking for information that cannot be shared with an outsider, which you are at the time.

Jigyāsa: "So much to talk about yourself and so cleverly that it leaves an impression!"

Veda: "Because you wish to beat the competition and grab the position of your choice."

Jigyāsa: "Feels amazing how few people are able to impress and influence masses, with their talk…"

 As Public Speaker

It must be a matter of great pride and privilege to have an opportunity to address public. While the gathering may be small or large and one may be a beginner or expert in public speaking, there are fresh expectations every time. Public speaking may be related to faith, politics, education, motivation, entertainment, performance etc. It can be prepared in advance or impromptu or a combination of both. Public speaking needs a lot of command on the context, subject, language and timing. Understanding the culture, perception and emotions of the audience is also equally important.

Public speaking has always been considered a great art, skill and ability to influence people, if conducted well. It takes a lot of practice and homework to appear before public and speak, whether for a short or long duration. Structuring once thoughts, choosing the right words, having the right eye contact, carrying a good amount of confidence and conviction, maintaining proper decorum of the event are a few essential elements of public speaking.

✓ Act responsible, positive, constructive and meaningful in your conversation and conduct.

✓ Be sure of the facts and figures that you share with the public at large.

✓ Observe the time allowed to you for speaking, so that other also get their chance.

✓ Express gratitude to and share credit with those who have made a contribution.

✓ Converse in a language which the gathering can understand and connect with.

✓ Stick to the agenda of the gathering and prepare well in advance.

✘ Getting late for the address and making people wait for you.

✘ Mixing too many subject / topics / points of talk to digress the agenda.

✘ Not having the right tools / equipment required, according to the size of gathering.

✘ Taking liberty at (mis)quoting facts / figures and thus misleading the people.

✘ Not making eye contact, whether it's a small gathering or a crowd.

✘ Going unprepared and taking too many pauses or interruptions to complete your talk.

Jigyâsa: "A lot of study, experience, skill and practice goes into making a great speaker."

Veda: "In order to become a great speaker, one needs to be a great listener and observer."

Jigyâsa: "I thought it just means to relax, enjoy and entertain yourself by listening or watching…"

 # As an Audience

Getting to listen to someone, whether an expert or amateur, is an opportunity to read someone's mind, thoughts, perceptions, ideas and talent. Every speaker comes up with certain expectations from the audience, whether support or cheer or silence. It all depends on the stage one is speaking on and the experience one has in public speaking. It may be a celebration, competition, announcement or any kind of gathering, which will define the type and mode of speaking. And the audience has to reciprocate accordingly.

As an audience, we expect something new, exciting, entertaining and inspiring from the speaker. Every speaker has a different ability to live up to our expectations. One must appreciate the fact that a speaker comes up with a lot of preparation, courage and hope. While, the today's world is of grabbing attention, rather than paying attention; as an audience, we are supposed to honor the speaker's opportunity. A good speaker can give us tips on how to speak, while a bad speaker denotes how not to speak.

✓ Reach the place in time and grab your place of choice / reservation.

✓ Be attentive and responsive to the speaker / performer.

✓ Maintain the discipline of sitting arrangement or queues at the venue.

✓ Keep unnecessary baggage out of the venue, since there won't be enough space to keep it.

✓ Ask your questions, if invited for / allowed, at you turn.

✓ Avoid cross talks / questions / confirmations to the speaker / performer / audience.

✗ Obstructing the view of others or the camera that is recording the speech / performance.

✗ Moving in and out of the hall / auditorium / theatre during the performance.

✗ Making noise, other than the reactions, which distracts or disturbs the performer / audience.

✗ Allowing children / mobile phone to create the unwarranted noise / disturbance.

✗ Engaging in activities beyond the performance and giving poor signals to the performer.

✗ Spilling food / beverages at the venue and making it difficult for the next user.

Jigyâsa: "Never realized that an audience can add so much value to self and the speaker."

Veda: "Listening carefully can always add value, as it enables both learning and feedback."

Jigyâsa: "Don't mind! But, I don't think there can be a good listening relationship with the in-laws..."

 As Mother-in-Law

While it is not meant to be a legal or legally binding designation, the English term sounds like that. Mother-in-laws, around the world, are (in) famous for constantly carrying a lethal, possessive and aggressive combination of generation gap, sense of insecurity and alter ego. It includes the mother-in-law of both a man and a woman. It is precisely because they lead the home affairs and are in the position to lead, guide, direct the actions of all at home. There is no chauvinism about it, but fathers-in-law are not known to be as powerful and difficult to manage.

As a mother-in-law, there is a lot of baggage and sense of governance that every woman bears in mind. For sure, that comes with a lot of experience and roller-coaster ride that she has gone through in her life. But, as the life moves on and the world around you change, you must also learn to change and adapt to the new ways of the younger generation, so as to connect and relate better with them. This will enable them to be more easy, open, compassionate and supportive towards you.

✓ Believe in your son / daughter-in-law's abilities and intentions to do good.

✓ Introduce and induct them into the family, with a lot of grace and honor.

✓ Appreciate their achievements and plans, while sharing your experiences to improve.

✓ Compliment her / his parents and try to play the same role with them.

✓ Protect / cover them from the undue criticism of other family members.

✓ Gradually give them due and deserving authority and responsibilities.

- ✗ Burdening them with a lot of expectations and demands, beyond their call of duty.

- ✗ Not allowing them the independence and decision-making power, needed for their role.

- ✗ Joining, provoking and feeding relatives for their criticism or humiliation.

- ✗ Making them feel inferior by constantly giving negative feedback.

- ✗ Trying to overpower their views, wishes and choices, with your thoughts and perceptions.

- ✗ Rejecting and challenging their abilities and achievements.

Jigyãsa: "I have really long time to actually become a mother-in-law. ha..ha..ha.."

Veda: "No doubt! However, not so long time to become a daughter-in-law."

Jigyãsa: "Don't' tell me! How will I manage so many responsibilities and expectations..."

 As Daughter / Son-in-Law

It's almost like being adopted once you are fully grown up. You have new parents who fully well understand that you are grown up and hence they have a long list of expectations from you. You are supposed to not only adapt to their lifestyle (may be temporarily or occasionally), but also learn and imbibe their ways of communication, dressing, food habits, culture etc. You willy-nilly become their brand ambassadors and models in the family and community that they belong to. May be that's the reasons why people insist their children to get married to a person who has these things in common.

It is rightfully assumed that you would understand the needs and comforts of your in-laws (not limited to the mother / father, but the entire family). It's indeed a task to build and sustain a positive and happy perception around you; irrespective of your efforts or achievements or success (before or after the marriage).

- ✓ Give them the same respect and support that you give to your parents.

- ✓ Earn their confidence, so that you are able to align them with yourself.

- ✓ Listen to them carefully and respond with a calm and constructive answer.

- ✓ Maintain and sustain their respect individually and in front of others.

- ✓ Make then your partner for decision-making in different personal / family matters.

- ✓ Accommodate few of their preferences with your likes of food, entertainment, celebration.

* Refusing their ideas / experience / suggestion, which may be insightful and helpful.

* Ill-treating them, whether physically or verbally, at home or in the presence of others.

* Ignoring their known preferences and thereby creating the environment of tussle.

* Avoiding their presence in the important events of celebration or family gathering.

* Differentiating / isolating them in terms of food, clothes and residence.

* Not taking care of their health needs, which come with the age.

Jigyāsa: "Got it! Being open and free of prejudices is a must in any relationship."

Veda: "Very nice! You are catching things pretty quickly and completely."

Jigyāsa: "Because I aspire to become a sportsperson. That allows both passion and fame, right..."

As a Sportsman

Full of flowing energy and willing to invest it into a sport, you must be looking at making it big by showing up your talent, skills, abilities and capacities. The sense of winning or making and breaking records must be far more superior and motivating than the certificates or medals that you get, as a token of those achievements. There is a great amount of constant focus, self-restraint, discipline, fitness and personal conduct that you must maintain at all times.

You may choose to engage with the sports at a professional level or just as a leisure / hobby. In both the situations, it's the sportsman spirit that makes you feel good about the sport and yourself. Sports are probably the most loved and adored activity, across the globe, with a huge amount of variety that one can choose to excel in. A sportsman can later become a coach or life coach, also. Besides being a sports person, you continue to be a human being, having your distinct personal and social needs.

✓ Always maintain your discipline of lifestyle to stay fit for the sport.

✓ Be open to sharing your success story and tips with the juniors.

✓ Conduct well in public life so that the public at large respect you and the sport.

✓ Carefully choose the products that you may be requested to endorse.

✓ Take due rest and avoid overdoing with your practice / performances.

✓ Gracefully appreciate the efforts and success of your fellow sportspersons.

* Running after money, rather than sustained and appreciable excellence.

* Endorsing products which are not true to their claim or harmful to the youngsters.

* Suffering with jealousy or envy of fellow sportspersons and shell locking yourself.

* Misbehaving on the ground or in public and tarnishing the image of self and the sport.

* Making controversial statements about the sport or your personal / public life.

* Taking the success for granted and not actively attempting to sustain it.

Jigyāsa: "Wonderful! Even a sportsperson has so much of influential power."

Veda: "Exactly! Every person, in whichever field, having fame and followers is influential."

Jigyāsa: "Must be a matter of great caution and responsibility for such a person..."

 As a Leader

Arguably the greatest human skill is being able to lead people. Leading people essentially is being able to bring together and drive a group of people into the same direction towards one common goal. One can be a natural leader or get trained into leadership. Like every other skill, this needs continuous learning and dynamism in responding to different kinds of situations. Leadership skill is itself a combination of lot of other skills like communication skill, people skill, strategic management skill, disaster management skill, public relations skills and much more. Sharper the combination is made and applied, the better leader you are.

Leadership is not only a great power but also an equally crucial responsibility. It takes a good amount of time and efforts to build one's image, persona and influence as a leader. However, it's so fragile that one single wrong incident or a few wrong words can spoil it to a great extent. Most of the well-known leaders have gone through both the experiences and managed to learn and sustain with grace.

✓ Lead by example of conduct, rather than by force of power or money.

✓ Constantly guide your people / team to focus on the organizational / common goal.

✓ Define the vision, mission and objectives with the collective inputs.

✓ Encourage people / team to participate and take situational leadership.

✓ Actively develop a second line of leadership or your succession plan.

✓ Have patience to listen to criticism or feedback and work upon it.

✘ Being autocratic and not allowing any diverse views / inputs / perspective.

✘ Misleading the team / people with statements or promises, without any real intentions.

✘ Not standing by the team / people in difficult / challenging situations.

✘ Not developing a successor and thus make the organization / objective weak in the long run.

✘ Showing poor conduct in public and hence letting the team / people down.

✘ Not having the plans in ambitious and clear ways, leading to ambiguity and loss of energy.

Jigyâsa: "Influencing essentially means the ability
to read the need and perceptions of people."

Veda: "Plus, define and deliver your thoughts,
actions, vision and communication accordingly."

Jigyâsa: "A good leader can actually reflect the
people and act on their behalf, isn't it..."

As a Representative

The opportunity, responsibility and pride of being a representative bring a lot of pressure also. One may get to represent a person, a family, a community, a culture, a class of people, a company or even a country. And, in each case, it must be earned through the sustained demonstration of skills, abilities, willingness, trust and experience. As a representative, one has to completely, correctly and carefully put forth the point of view or the abilities of the person / entity being represented. Representative may choose to be one or it may be a matter or chance or force.

Once a representative, is always a representative. Even if not acting in the same capacity, people continue to recognize and perceive them as such. Therefore, it is not just one event or occasion where one must behave with utmost caution and consciousness but continue to do so in one's public life later also. It includes making the right disclosures and statements, at the right time, which requires a lot of preparation and understanding of the role and responsibility, in advance.

✓ Understand your role, responsibilities and limits of the authority.

✓ Act sensibly and within your defined limitations as a representative.

✓ Attempt to maintain / sustain the respect, pride, reputation of whom you represent.

✓ Exercise extra caution when you are not an official representative but assumed as such.

✓ Clarify to the organization / person and public, if you don't wish to be looked at like this.

✓ Articulate well or seek time to respond, when not sure about the correct position to take.

✘ Delegating the right to representation without the consent / order / consultation.

✘ Breaking any law while acting in the capacity of a representative.

✘ Making decisions or giving statements beyond the authority extended to you.

✘ Indulging into misconduct and thereby risking the reputation / interests.

✘ Going unprepared to make a representation, thus failing the whole purpose.

✘ Not inviting a discussion in unforeseen or uncertain situations and taking solemn calls.

Jigyâsa: "There are so many dimensions to each role that any person may occupy."

Veda: "Correct. With each such dimension, a change or adjustment in the approach is required."

Jigyâsa: "Personalities and positions are two dimensions to it. Can a place also add..."

SEGMENT C : POSITION RELATED

St. Mary's School
7 til' late GROCER
STOP

Jigyâsa: "You mean to say that I also need to be
watchful of where I am!"

Veda: "Yes, the place, venue or location will also
add or define the rules of conduct."

Jigyâsa: "Does that apply to even a place of
sheer recreation..."

 # At a Playground

Public, private, indoor, outdoor, equipped or not, well organized or just a make-shift arrangement to facilitate a game / play / sport, a playground is a source of sheer energy, fun, excitement and enthusiasm for many. As we grow older, we get to spend lesser time at a playground. Yet, just the thought of being there and participate in game, fills us with a lot of zeal, readiness to give it our best and an urge to win. It brings the child alive, in one and all. It may or may not be flocked by other players, coaches, referees, viewers, media persons etc.

Despite all the different sources, modes and types of entertainment that the mankind has invented so far, playgrounds continue to constantly attract the greatest of crowds, in the form of participants or supporters. In fact, there is a whole form of entertainment that depends upon the playgrounds. Playgrounds are also the sources of great amount of employment and revenues. Everyone present at the playground or involved in preparing it actually contributes towards the game.

✓ Wait for your (or your child's) turn and share the common time / facilities.

✓ Seek permission to bring people who are not normally allowed at or using the playground.

✓ Take care of the sports stuff / eatables that you bring to the playground.

✓ Restore the equipment / facility, before leaving; if not taken care by a support staff.

✓ Follow the instructions of usage and timing of the playground to remain open.

✓ Vacate the place as per the defined timing of the playground or your reserved time.

✖ Littering the place with eatables / wrappers / waste papers or plastic.

✖ Creating unnecessary noise while playing, that is beyond the normal playful voices.

✖ Entering an argument with others for using the common time / place / game.

✖ Obstructing or damaging the facilities and hence causing issues to the next user.

✖ Leaving your stuff / baggage there and wasting others' time to find it later.

✖ Bringing unauthorized / unapproved people or friends to the playground.

Jigyãsa: "Can't take even a place of play for granted. Need to know and respect our limits."

Veda: "That's because you are not alone there. There are others too with similar rights & expectations."

Jigyãsa: "Isn't it the case with every place where many people are present..."

 At Public Places

Almost impossible to list the public places, which have also entered another dimension of the virtual world now. However, in the virtual world, we can always decide on what is public and what is not. Public places are almost always surrounded by a number of strangers. People come there alone or with family or friends or colleagues. The purpose of all the people present there, may be similar, since most of the public places are meant for a particular objective. Such places may be developed and maintained by a government or an NGO or a philanthropist.

Public places facilitate us for large gatherings and collective participation in certain regular or occasional events or activities. Such places may be open to all or selective people and may be free of charge or demand a fee. At times, private places can be turned into a public place, for a temporary purpose. Being at a public place is so frequent and common in our lives that we might not even realize being there. Most of the public places have clearly defined and displayed rules of conduct.

✓ Maintain silence or speak at a normal voice pitch, to avoid unnecessary embarrassment.

✓ Park the vehicle, if any, at the prescribed place and pay the due fee.

✓ Abide by the rules / code of conduct of the place and cooperate with the admin staff.

✓ Avoid turning into a crowd, by standing and walking in defined queues / spaces.

✓ Follow the safety / security rules of the place and cooperate with the security staff.

✓ Keep the place clean, peaceful and pleasant, when you are there and when you leave.

✗ Staying there for longer than the allowed / open time, as per the security measures.

✗ Making unwarranted noise and disturbing others who are there for individual purposes.

✗ Not maintaining the cleanliness / hygiene of the place, by throwing garbage there.

✗ Causing inconvenience to others by violating the order of parking / sitting / waiting.

✗ Manufacturing unusual attraction / distraction to the people present and leading to havoc.

✗ Spreading security related rumors or violating the security norms.

Jigyâsa: "Whether a common purpose or not, but public places have common access to all."

Veda: "And that access must be appreciated and respected by one and all."

Jigyâsa: "Thank God! There are no such rules of behavior back home..."

At Home

The most comfortable, lovable and peaceful place in the world. Or, at least, it is supposed to be. It's not just a covered shelter, but also the habitat of emotions, care and ever-growing memories. Quite metaphorically, it is said that a family turns a house into a home. Which emphasizes on how essential emotions are, in addition to the sand and iron that are used to build a house. It's a home where we grow and learn all the early lessons of our lives. Home gives us the comfort to relax and feel safe, with which we can gradually prepare ourselves to face the bigger external world.

In fact, it's a matter of great fortune to have a home, which the unfortunate homeless people can testify, more than anyone else. At times, those born with the privilege of having a home, take it for granted and fail to value its existence, importance and significance. Depending upon the wealth of the owner of a home, it may be tiny or small or big or even grand. However, having a home is far more crucial than its size, shape and structure.

✓ Follow the order and arrangement of things and put those back from where you took.

✓ Respect the privacy of all the family members / roomies staying there with you.

✓ Inform everyone if you are inviting someone home, even if for a short while.

✓ Consult with all before changing / adjusting the arrangement of furniture / other things.

✓ Fix a place and time for your creative interests, so that others don't get impacted.

✓ Regularly conduct some deep cleaning / dusting / washing of the household stuffs.

✘ Not respecting the rule of home, about when to come and leave.

✘ Inviting and entertaining unexpected guests, to leave others at home in a fix.

✘ Disturbing the order, by not putting things back in place or shifting their place.

✘ Piling up stacks of clothes or utensils to wash and making it difficult to sustain life.

✘ Not throwing garbage out of home, at the right time and regularly.

✘ Not doing the necessary maintenance and upkeep of the home, as and when needed.

Jigyâsa: "Just never expected this. Even at home we need to behave and maintain decorum."

Veda: "That's simply to ensure the comfort of home is sustained for you and others."

Jigyâsa: "Whenever I think of comfort, I think of flying high and watching the clouds..."

 # During a Flight

Still a dream to come true for a lot of people in the world, but almost everyone is at least aware of it. Flight is the fastest mode of mass travel available to the humanity. And, the most time taking in terms of boarding and de-boarding. Flights and the airports are apparently far more sophisticated and organized than the other modes of transport, while the others are also catching up in many ways. Though the rules, protocols and procedures applicable to the flights and airports may remain significantly stricter and critical to follow. Simply because it is all about flying at some thousand's feet height.

Flights are a matter of amusement for those who don't get a chance to board any. They prove to be extremely exciting for the first-time flyers or the relatively infrequent flyers. However, the frequent flyers are often found neither excited nor quite happy about the flights, irrespective of the economy or business class that they happen to travel in. A person who hasn't boarded a flight may wonder what these terms mean.

✓ Carefully reach your seat, without stomping on anyone's foot or knees.

✓ Carry a hand baggage which is tidy and safe to keep in the prescribed place.

✓ Listen to and follow the safety instructions, on each occasion.

✓ Reach out to the flight crew for any clarification or support required.

✓ Cooperate with the fellow passengers if they need to move into / out of their seats.

✓ Patiently wait for your turn to board and deboard the flight.

✗ Asking people to exchange their seat with you so that you can be comfortable.

✗ Stealing the safety instruction card / magazine from the flight seat.

✗ Not following the safety instructions / directions by the flight crew or captain.

✗ Spilling food / beverages / water on the seat or floor of the flight.

✗ Making noise, either by talking loudly or through your electrical gadgets.

✗ Pushing your hand baggage too much against that of others or into their legs.

Jigyâsa: "There is so much to learn and follow beyond what the flight crew tells us."

Veda: "Flights are the most expensive, fast, sophisticated and security intense mode of travel."

Jigyâsa (chuckles): "However, with the smallest or say the most compact of facilities..."

 # At Public Toilets

Here is a place which is strictly private in its use, but actually public. A facility that is built and/ or maintained by the government administration or any non-government organization. A place which is sought after by one and all, when nature calls. Irrespective of who we are and what we do, it's an indispensable necessity, so far as we continue to eat and drink. Even if few people are opulent enough to almost never face the need of using a public toilet, the masses will always need and appreciate having it. Public toilets are of the utmost need, whether stand alone or at any other public place.

Depending upon the economic and social status of a country, public toilets can be found. Or say, public toilets reflect the economic and social status of a country. The usage of a public toilet is a responsibility, as much as a right. There is no limit or end to the users of a public toilet, which every user must be aware of and conscious about. Public toilets give the quickest lessons on 'behave the way you want others to behave'.

✓ Use the toilet as per the style (western or otherwise) and built of the toilet.

✓ Wait for another user to finish and come out, rather than banging on the door.

✓ Keep it locked when you are using it, to avoid embarrassment to self and others.

✓ Keep the toilet clean, dry and safe for the next user to come.

✓ Make due payment to the maintenance staff, if it's not a free facility.

✓ Ask for a help, rather than attempting a non-sustainable make-shift arrangement.

✗ Spilling water around and making it difficult for the other users.

✗ Spending unnecessary time inside it and troubling other users.

✗ Putting obscene posters / remarks on the walls of the public toilet.

✗ Leaving it dirty / unclean and increasing pressure on the maintenance staff.

✗ Arguing not to make the prescribed payment, for usage of the facility.

✗ Damaging the water supply, sanitary ware, light or door of the toilet.

Jigyāsa: "It's so easy to take the public toilets
            for granted, which we must not."

Veda: "Since we go there when there is no other
            alternate and everyone does it."

Jigyāsa: "What are the other things that a lot
            of people get to participate in..."

 During Festivals

Those frequent, lovely and much awaited shots of energy, excitement and collective celebrations. While things may not be hunky-dory around us and we may have difference kinds of challenges and difficulties in life, festivals bring us some contagious happiness and bliss. That breeze of fresh surrounding zeal can bring joy and thrill to anyone. Festivals always demand for a lot of preparations and post celebration work also, which is executed like a project by a team of people.

Festivals not only invoke a lot of creativity, in the ways of celebration, but also support the economy in the dimmest of situations. Festivals are closely attached to the deep-rooted culture and traditions of the respective community. Which makes it all the most compulsory to celebrate it in the finest way possible. In that course, festivals support a lot of small and big industries, in terms of business. Festivals are mostly looked at as an event of spend and earning, which encourages the entire market for production, distribution and consumption.

✓ Join the celebration with the full of your energy and best dressing possible.

✓ Greet others, whether personally or through mass / social media messages, on the festival.

✓ Be careful of not hurting yourself or others, as you enjoy the festival.

✓ Make your plan and preparation, well in advance, along with friends & family.

✓ Be generous in sharing things with those who can't afford to celebrate, on their own.

✓ Spread good social messages and awareness, as relevant / relatable to the festival.

✗ Making fun of a festival, whether it belongs to your community or not.

✗ Going overboard with the celebrations and thus disturbing / irritating others.

✗ Isolating oneself from the celebrations, which may turn down the mood of others.

✗ Not appreciating the way others wish to enjoy and celebrate the festival.

✗ In the attempt to modernize, spoiling the feel and spirit of the festival.

✗ Not allowing leaves to your employees / staff, to celebrate and spend time with family.

Jigyâsa: "That's an absolutely fresh perspective
about how to celebrate festivals."

Veda: "You will get to learn a lot of new
perspective as you grow, and your responsibilities
grow."

Jigyâsa: "I know what you are trying to hint at.
I will be waiting for such an occasion..."

 In Family Events

A gathering of a lot of known and unknown faces, who belong to the same family or extended family. It may be an event of celebration or condolence, which may be planned or otherwise. Such gatherings may be wishful or compulsory to attend. There are organizers who remain busy making the arrangements, the fun makers who are in the state of constant enjoyment and those who are just not interested in the event but forced into that irrelevant incidence and boredom. While it's an opportunity for many to create and rejuvenate both the relations and network, those who are bored cannot relate to it.

Events may last from few hours to few days. Some attendees may attend it for the complete duration and other may stay there partly. Depending upon the number of people joining the event, the type of occasion and the affordability of those organizing it; budget of the event will vary. Accordingly, the venue and arrangements will be managed. All the attendees of such event are supposed to subscribe to the same and adjust their expectations accordingly.

✓ Give a helping hand in whatever task you can support to complete.

✓ Prepare yourself in time for the event(s) and also help others.

✓ Appreciate the work / efforts / preparation done by others to make it happen.

✓ Reach out to the known or unknown people and greet them well.

✓ Rejuvenate old memories with the family members who are meeting after long time.

✓ As per capacity of organizer, be reasonable in your expectations of the arrangements.

* Throwing tantrums and demanding things of a particular type or form.

* Making your own plans out of the event, making others wonder what you are up to.

* Showing no interest in the event and in meeting the family / relatives.

* Attending the even in a casual manner, rather than being prepared for it.

* Not supporting or helping in the preparations or execution of the tasks.

* Creating awkward and uncomfortable moments during the event, for others.

Jigyāsa: "Taking active part in those responsibilities must be fun and learning."

Veda: "Indeed! Whatever we learn in the family events, can help and guide us in our professional life too."

Jigyāsa: "And the most fun part is to plan for and go buy the stuff required for the event…"

 # During Shopping

Whether you do it for necessities or as a pastime or as a stress buster, shopping is a part of our daily life. After going online, shopping has actually become a daily event, quite literally. Even if you don't place the order and pay online, adding to a wishlist or cart is no less than actual shopping and/or window shopping. Or say, at least it gives the feeling of buying something or exploring something to buy. While online shopping is an absolutely private affair, shopping offline or in the market actually means being at a public place too.

Shopping essentially includes negotiations, which depends upon your budget, experience, knowledge of pricing, type of market and relation with the vendor. Offline shopping involves a huge amount of negotiation, even in repeated buying. However, on the other side, online shopping hardly allows any kind of negotiation. Even the branded stores, departmental stores and supermarkets do not encourage negotiations. In a nutshell, it can be concluded that customers / consumers negotiate where they can.

✓ Make your selection criteria clear to help the shopkeeper show you the right items.

✓ Define you budget range, in alignment with the choice of type of product.

✓ Wait for your turn, if the shopkeeper / cashier is already busy with another customer.

✓ Carry your shopping bag to avoid unnecessary consumption of single use plastic.

✓ Keep the necessary change with you or make payments through online modes.

✓ Appreciate the hospitality, if any, offered by the staff / shopkeeper.

✖ Negotiating the price even when it is not allowed or appreciated by the shopkeeper.

✖ Asking for too many varieties or products to be shown, which you don't intend to buy.

✖ Doing window-shopping as a pastime and wasting the time / energy of shopkeeper.

✖ Chit-chatting in the shop and blocking the space to not allow other customers.

✖ Abusing the facilities provided in the shop and being unapologetic about it.

✖ Stealing things from a shop i.e. sneaking those without making the due payment.

Jigyāsa: "That's a bit too much now. Shopping must be free of any rules."

Veda: "Ha..Ha..Ha.. those are rules but sheer recommendations to conduct yourself well."

Jigyāsa: "Yeah! Now I have started wondering what next place is coming my way..."

 Places of Worship

Since time immemorial, mankind has been looking forward to the supreme power, which is behind the creation, operation and demolition of this great universe. A universe which is still far beyond our knowledge and only known to some extent with a mix a scientific tools and imagination. It is a place of worship where all of the believers go and seek their peace of mind, healing, faith, blessings and solutions; depending upon their respective beliefs.

Places of worship normally conduct several kinds of routine and occasional activities, which are meant for and instrumental to the enhancement of devotion in the people. Such activities are deep routed in the culture of the respective believers and thus travel from, or say are transmitted from, one generation to another. Places of worship are not just the centers of spiritual emotions and philosophical exchanges, but also the regular boosters of economic activities. Simply because there are a lot of commercial activities attached to, initiated by and dependent on those.

✓ Follow the code / instructions of attire, footwear and the accessories, if any.

✓ Stay in the queue of devotees and keep moving as per the order / instructions.

✓ Stay calm and make no noise, other than joining the mass chanting / prayers.

✓ Avoid moving out of the place while some activity / procession in underway.

✓ Accept and have the Prasad (share of offerings), which is distributed amongst all.

✓ Participate in the tasks there or make service to the place of worship.

*   Going there even when you don't have respect / faith / belief in the place.

*   Avoiding any participation in the rituals being carried out there.

*   Staying busy in your electronic devices or chats to disturb the proceedings there.

*   Refusing to follow the code of conduct or the dress code prescribed for the place.

*   Criticizing or arguing (not seeking to understand) with the priests or people.

*   Breaking the order of standing / walking, which leads to mismanagement.

Jigyâsa: "While I am yet to understand devotion, I fully agree to this piece of advice."

Veda: "God bless you, baby! Devotion will come to you when you surrender and seek."

Jigyâsa: "You know what! My first prayer always comes for my tummy and I am very hungry..."

 # At Food Outlets

Just another dine-out or a quick bite of your favorite snack or a friendly treat or a party, food outlets have increasingly become a part of our life. More and more for the people staying in cities and towns. Food outlets may be found in many different sizes, from a temporary and moveable serving stall or wagon to a posh restaurant / hotel. And they serve a range of specialized and/or general dishes. Whether operated as a matter of passion, mixed with the livelihood or just as an option of earning, food outlets are a source and destination of joy.

Depending upon the quality, consistency, flavor and service; many a food outlets have made it really big and become a brand. As the brand grows, increases the specialization and the responsibility to serve better and also the competition. The customers of any food outlet, whether loyal or experimental, are always looking for a value for money. And that comes from the combined package of taste, experience, service and convenience. In fact, this combination is what defines the value of what they have to offer.

✓ Request and ensure advance reservations, if you wish to visit in a large number.

✓ Take time to decide your choice and place order at once, rather than repeating.

✓ Help yourself if the outlet doesn't have serving facility, but self-serve mode.

✓ Being courteous and kind to the serving staff and support staff.

✓ Check your bill properly and clarify any doubt on order or price.

✓ Avoid wasting food and money by excessively ordering, in excitement.

✗ Ordering something which the outlet doesn't even prepare and serve.

✗ Giving a tip to the waiter(s), when it isn't allowed or appreciated.

✗ Spilling food / beverages and making it tough for the housekeeping staff.

✗ Allowing kids to wander around and mess up things for the staff / other customers.

✗ Insisting on a mode of payment, which they don't facilitate / entertain.

✗ Stealing their cutlery or other accessories or seeking complimentary food items.

Jigyāsa (while munching on her snacks): "My yummy mummy! You must open a food outlet. I will manage it."

Veda (laughs): "Why not! However, we will not allow you to eat there."

Jigyāsa (cunningly suggests): "Then I will have to go for a movie and have my lunch there..."

 At a Movie Theatre

Unlike other public places, all present at a movie theatre are there for one common purpose. On a lighter note, there may be a few exceptions like someone there to take a peaceful nap in air-conditioned environment or someone just trying to hide from others and hence taking advantage of the constant darkness. In the field of entertainment, movie theatres have taken a great lead, world over. May be just next to the stadiums for sports. The larger than life experience that a movie theatre provides, is truly unparallel and thus attracts so many people.

Movie theatres are also found in different shapes and sizes, from single screen to multiplexes and from stand alone to a part of a shopping mall. Irrespective of that, there are written and assumed rules or protocols of being and behaving at a theatre. However, depending upon the size, type and location of a theatre, one may find very different kinds of people coming and enjoying movies at a theatre, in comparison to another. Home theatres are strictly private, by the way.

✓ Find your seat and settle there well within time, both before start and after the interval.

✓ Abide by the rules of the theatre, with respect to the allowed baggage.

✓ Ignore small voices and thus avoid an argument with the fellow viewers.

✓ Be careful not to obstruct anyone's view or audio of the movie.

✓ Keep your ticket(s) handy to show to the staff at the entry or during the show.

✓ Patiently and orderly move to the Emergency door, in case of unexpected events.

✗ Moving in and out of the theatre while the movie is being projected.

✗ Getting toddlers to the theatre, who aren't comfortable there and make it so for others.

✗ Leaving the seat(s) dirty or damaged, as you exit the theatre.

✗ Interrupting / disturbing the view / experience of others, with your phone rings / chats.

✗ Stomping on co-viewers feet, while walking in / out of your seat.

✗ Getting into an argument with the co-viewers and disturbing the entire gathering.

Jigyāsa: "I have actually faced such people who don't behave well at a movie theatre."

Veda: "Whenever and wherever you face such things, tell them politely what we have discussed."

Jigyāsa: "I really wish I could share all of this with my friends and acquintances, over social media..."

 # At Social Media

That another world where many of us are present in many ways, characters, avatars and profiles. Every social media is meant for a different expression, networking, updates, voice, sharing and promotion. It has not only surfaced and supported a lot of social, economic and humanitarian issues; but also created a lot of public figures or stars or celebrities. For that matter, it has become a necessity for all the public figures and celebrities to have their constant presence at different social media platforms.

Social media has always received mixed feedback or reactions, in terms of whether it helps or spoils and whether it's fair or biased. It is a tool which can help you connect, learn and present. It is up to a user how to use it or abuse it. Every such platform has their own privacy and content related policy that binds every user and the platform also. Social media has become the next level of communication amongst a large population around the world, simply because it goes far beyond the written and/or verbal communication, which is high speed also.

✓ Share inspirational posts or things that make others feel good and happy.

✓ Utilize the forum to connect with friends and family, who are not living in proximity.

✓ Follow the people and pages that you find good to learn from or draw inspiration.

✓ Learn the technology and how others use it to make impressive posts.

✓ Respond to the people who react to your posts, whether known to you or not.

✓ Carefully select the audience and secrecy for your posts, whether public or private.

✖ Sharing / forwarding posts without knowing their authenticity or validation.

✖ Ignoring the people who wish to connect with you or react to your posts.

✖ Getting into never ending debates with anyone, which is visible to all on social media.

✖ Pestering someone with unsolicited and unwanted personal messages.

✖ Spreading rumors / superstition / fake news and negatively influencing others.

✖ Soliciting likes / comments / shares from people unknown, to win a competition.

Jigyâsa: "Oh yes! How could we miss what and how to do on social media!"

Veda: "Social media is a tool and it always depends on what a user does with it."

Jigyâsa: "In the same way, is it correct to say that office is a tool to build our career…"

 At Workplace

Where most of us engage, whether physically or virtually, in order to earn our livelihood. We may be there in the capacity of an owner or an employee. For the small-time street vendors and like people, a workplace may be mobile also. Going strictly by the definition, even a house is a workplace for both the homemakers and the aids. However, homemakers don't get paid for it. We may or may not have colleagues and/or teams there. There may be a formal or informal training to get onboarded, added by a qualification and/or experience.

Workplace not only forms a major part of our life and mental space, but also is essential to our life. Moving from one workplace to another is an also an interesting phenomenon, largely exclusive to the people in service. Depending upon the different types of workplaces, those are governed with different kinds of laws. With the technological advancement around the world, a notable change and creativity have arrived in the scope, size, shape and surrounding of the workplace.

✓ Welcome the new colleagues and help them gel with the culture and team.

✓ Clarify doubts for self and others, to avoid any rumors or misinformation.

✓ Participate in the employee engagement activities and help build a good culture.

✓ Cooperate and support in maintaining the upkeep and good shape of infrastructure.

✓ Be an ambassador of the organization culture, to the external world.

✓ Take highest care of the office information and ensure zero leakage of the same.

x   Abusing the entertainment / refreshment / gaming or recreation facilities.

x   Getting friendly with those colleagues who are actually not comfortable with that.

x   Hiding and taking advantage of personal relations at the workplace.

x   Submitting fake bills of expenses for taking a reimbursement from the office.

x   Making loud / harsh arguments with colleagues, in open spaces of the office.

x   Taking home things that don't belong to you or more than what you are entitled to.

Jigyāsa: "Office can be a source of enrichment or stress, depending upon how we act there."

Veda: "Wonderful! I am sure very seasoned professionals would appreciate your statement."

Jigyāsa: "Till the time I get to work, an office is just an imagination, like a foreign land..."

 # At Foreign Trips

Whether the visa is pre-approved or on arrival and whether it's for tourism, business, occupation, study or shift of place of stay, being in a foreign country can make anybody nervous and cautious. More so, when someone happens to be there for the first time. At a foreign land, one must constantly carry the knowledge / support of the local language, awareness of the local laws / customs, a taste for the local delicacies or flavor, sufficient money to sustain & enjoy the stay and a valid passport.

Any person at a foreign land, whether temporary or permanent, is often identified and treated as a representative of the country of one's origin. It goes without saying and backed up by law also, till the time a person gets to become a citizen of the foreign country. These days it's another fashion or trend to attend weddings at a foreign land, whether as a destination wedding or the wedding of a friend who is a foreigner. In any case, the one thing to be careful at a foreign land is to not offend or hurt anyone.

✓ Prepare well for the culture, language, currency and temperature of that country.

✓ Keep your original passport along, whether at the place of residence of outside.

✓ Stay in touch with the national consulate for any issues of citizenship or passport.

✓ Have a friend / colleague / acquaintance to help you out with the place.

✓ Keep a local phone / mobile connection to stay connected with the friends / family.

✓ Have and follow your itinerary of work, travel, leisure and shopping.

* Roaming around without your passport and/or not being able to produce the same.

* Travelling alone when you don't know the people and their language.

* Violating the rules / laws / customs of the place and falling into unnecessary trouble.

* Not having a defined agenda / timeline and not being able to conclude the trip accordingly.

* Getting into things beyond the permissible acts, as per the VISA that was granted to you.

* Misbehaving with the people and hence end up bringing bad name to your own country.

Jigyâsa: "While I crave for going on a foreign trip, there is a lot that I wish to finish first."

Veda: "I know. You wish to visit all the tourist places that we have here in Bharat."

Jigyâsa: "Exactly! What great fun it will be with a lot of history, spirituality and nature..."

 At Tourist Places

Irrespective of the location or destination or the frequency and occasion of being there, tourist places are not just public places but the places with a large number of people gathered for leisure and those who provide services to such people. Tourist places are mostly the sought-after locations for vacation and/or relaxation. One may choose to go there alone or with friends or as a couple or in a larger group. And the destination is mostly chosen according to that. Tourism can often be combined with the few other events or purposes; like sports, medication, family events, research, exploration, education etc.

People don't prefer to visit the same tourist place again, unless they missed a few important attractions there. However, they inspire others to visit that place, through the word of mouth and also the word of social media. This trend has increased multifold with the like increase in usage of both camera (including mobile camera) and the social media for sharing those moments.

✓ Plan well on what you wish to do or visit and in how much time.

✓ Calculate your budget, well in advance, including the stay, travel, food and shopping.

✓ Follow the instructions of your guide or the rules of that place.

✓ Constantly take care of your valuables and other stuff that you carry along.

✓ Be respectful to the spiritual / historical / moral or scientific importance of the place.

✓ Assist strangers at the place, if they need help or guidance regarding the place or otherwise.

✖ Wandering at unknown / unexplored places and risking your safety.

✖ Exhausting your resources and seeking monetary help from strangers.

✖ Leaving the place dirty / unkempt or making it unworthy for the other travelers.

✖ Damaging the property / beauty / heritage of the place and fleeing away.

✖ Misleading people about the whereabouts of the place and causing undue discomfort.

✖ Getting too friendly with strangers and seeking / accepting their company.

Jigyāsa: "You know what Mumma! Mumma knows it all. Quite literally."

Veda (gives a long tight hug): "Only when the child cares, shares and listens to Mumma."

Jigyāsa: "I wonder how I will remember and recall all of it when in need. I wish someone writes a book..."

The Sober AUTHOR

Name: Pratik 'Bharat' Palor *(Darpan)*
Born to: Mrs. Anita & Mr. Pramod Palor
Accompanied by: Manisha (Wife),
Shree & Vallari (Daughters)
Gifted with Life on: 27-06-1987
Committed the Seven Lives on: 16-01-2011
Education: CA (Gold Medalist) and
CS (All India Seventh Rank)
Whatsapp: +91-7829003200
YouTube Channel: प्रतीक भारत पलोड़ – reflectionpoet
Facebook Page: दर्पण – reflectionpoet
Instagram: @poet_pratik

Literary Contributions

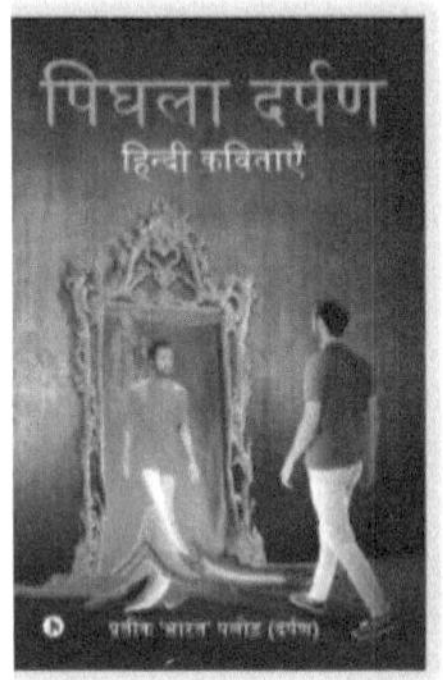

A man of less words is a Poet. And here is a collection of Poetry written by an introspective, reflective and positive man. Poetry that makes you dive deep within and realize the feelings that are pushed beneath many covers of the outer world. Embark upon the soul-searching journey, along with the Poet, and stay mesmerized with the magic of his experiments with words.

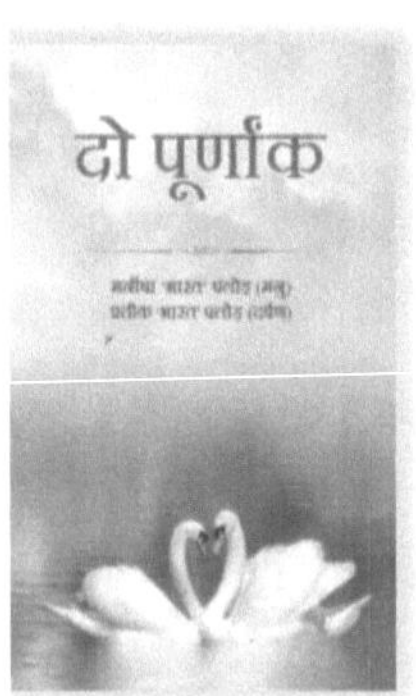

Stories that will make you feel, introspect and change. Stories that touch you deep inside and urge that sleeping sentiment to rise and embrace you. Stories that are pretty off-beat, and yet feel like your own. Stories that are daring, honest and hard hitting. Stories that are a mix of experiences and imagination and wishes and guilt.

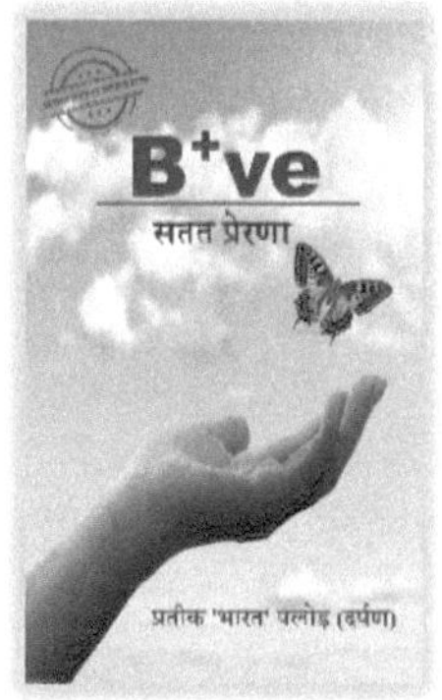

Being positive is not about attempting and changing everything around us, but it is accepting the people, situations and things as they are, with the grit and will to do better every time. The book doesn't show you the path to sure success, but the ways to remain happy and keep going.

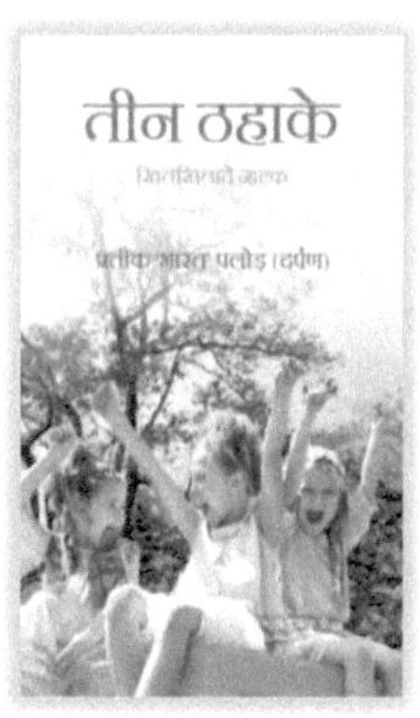

Plays that would take you to another world where nothing looks like seen, felt or imagined before. The world of extraordinary and over the top characters, which are still relevant and not to be forgotten. The dialogues that are most unconventional and, hence refreshing. The messages that are hidden and still very deep and strong.

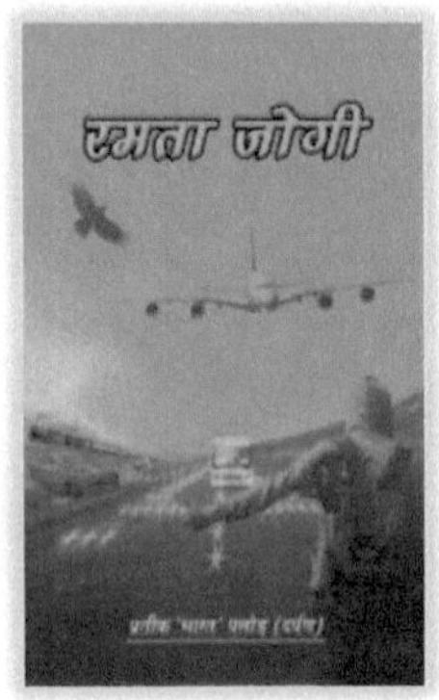

A book on Journeys, which is not yet another Travelogue. A book where the means and ways of journey are more important and prominent than the destinations. It takes the reader to an experience ride of emotions, ranging from childhood to teenage to youth and finally to married life. A book that takes you down the cultural lane of BHARAT.

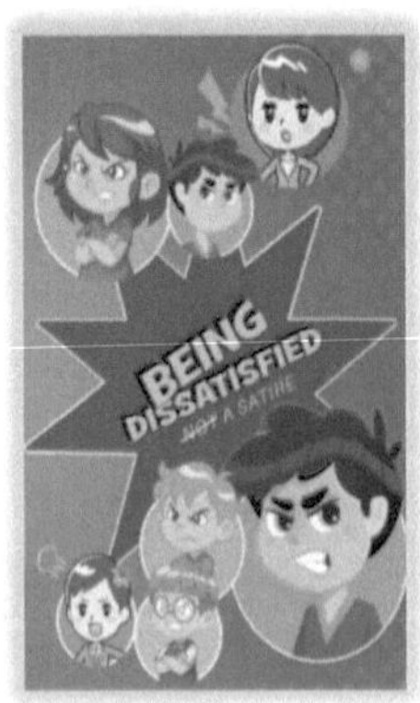

If you feel that this book will somehow give you a solution to any of your problems, sorry but that's neither the intent nor the content. This book, with the most unheard (or say awkward) of name and soul, will lead you to realize how deeply and sincerely the Author wishes you to understand your own expectations from the world, including yourself, and stay DISSATISFIED for Life.

Known to be a thorough gentleman, well behaved and animated personality, Pratik has been a role model of mannerism for the people around him. Be it home or office or community or an absolutely new place, Pratik knows how to conduct himself and secure the best of relations with people. He knows when and how and with whom to express or hold his emotions. Through a long practical experience gained from the people around, he has attained the ability to sense the situation and react (rather respond) accordingly. His calm, choice of words and pleasant appearance helps him win both people and arguments. His excellent academic, professional and literary career only adds to his humbleness and never overshadows his humility.